Heather
and the Angels

Do you believe in angels? Have you actually ever seen an angel or felt the presence of an angel? Ancient manuscripts say that angels who visit us on earth are messengers of God. I believe in angels. Perhaps after you read this story you will too.

E. LINDA CUSHNER

LitPrime Solutions
21250 Hawthorne Blvd
Suite 500, Torrance, CA 90503
www.litprime.com
Phone: 1-800-981-9893

Published by LitPrime Solutions   06/13/2023

ISBN: 979-8-88703-203-0(sc)
ISBN: 979-8-88703-269-6(hc)
ISBN: 979-8-88703-204-7(e)

Library of Congress Control Number: 2023904226

This book is dedicated to my family and friends and all who encouraged me to continue writing. Especially to my sister-in law, Barbara who is now with the angels. Our families shared so many joyful and wonderful holidays in the beautiful state of Vermont.

CONTENTS

Acknowledgement ix

Chapter One: Heather 1
Chapter Two: Heather and Jamie 3
Chapter Three: Sara 6
Chapter Four: Elizabeth and Sara 9
Chapter Five: Charlie 12
Chapter Six: Charlie and Sara 15
Chapter Seven: Life in Vermont 17
Chapter Eight: Jonathon 20
Chapter Nine: Charlie 22
Chapter Ten: Jonathon...24
Chapter Eleven: Adventures 26
Chapter Twelve: Thanksgiving 29
Chapter Thirteen: Mysterious 31
Chapter Fourteen: Waiting 33
Chapter Fifteen: Changes...36
Chapter Sixteen: Bits and Pieces..38
Chapter Seventeen: Plans 40
Chapter Eighteen: Three Long Days.....................................43
Chapter Nineteen: Saddness 44

Chapter Twenty: Why God? 47

Chapter Twenty-One: Different Life..........................49

Chapter Twenty-Two: Growing Up 51

Chapter Twenty-Three: Surprises! 52

Chapter Twenty-Four: Paul 55

Chapter Twenty-Five: New Plans 59

Chapter Twenty-Six: Friendship...............................63

Chapter Twenty-Seven: Decisions 65

Chapter Twenty-Eight: Life Moves On.....................67

Chapter Twenty-Nine: Confession............................69

Chapter Thirty: Present...72

Chapter Thirty-One: New Relationships 76

Chapter Thirty-Two: The Future 78

ACKNOWLEDGEMENT

MY SPECIAL THANKS TO THE Episcopal Church which has been so instrumental in guiding my journey here on earth.

For He will command his angels concerning you,
to guard you in all your ways.
On their hands, they will bear you up,
so that you will not hit your foot against a stone.

CHAPTER ONE

Heather

I T IS DECEMBER IN VERMONT. The softly falling snow is creating a white tapestry that is gently covering the little town of Westford. Holiday lights that decorate the main street are twinkling and playing peekaboo in the wintry haze. All is still. All is quiet. Suddenly a figure appears in the moonlit, silvery sky over the southern mountains that look down into the little town. The figure unfurls what appear to be feathery wings and begins to glide across the heavens toward the horizon just outside Westford. Gently and slowly, the figure comes to rest on the earth's surface, landing once, twice and then it is gone fading into the panorama of the whirling, drifting snow.

At this precise moment, sixteen-year-old Heather Burbank is gazing dreamily out of the window in her bedroom. Perhaps her peripheral vision has caught a glimpse of a gossamer figure gliding across the sky. Perhaps at one time, she might have continued to search the heavens for another glimpse of this shadowy figure, thinking perhaps that it could have been an angel or a spirit or some other heavenly creature; but sadly, she turns away because she no longer believes in angels.

"There is nothing there," she whispered to herself. However, in the back of her mind, she begins to doubt and thinks that perhaps she should continue to look out the window and pursue the path of this strange hazy figure; but then she decidedly shakes her head and whispers again, "No, there are no angels, because if there were angels, then Dad would still be here with us."

Her mind wanders back to a different time and space. She hears her father's voice as he ruffled her hair and winked at her with those clear green eyes and said, "Hi, angel, what kinds of plans do you have for your life today?" She sees him picking up her little brother and holding him way up over his head, and she sees her little brothers legs wiggling around and hears her brother's chirpy giggles as he looks down at his father.

"Heather," her mother's voice calls from the bottom of the stairs, interrupting her melancholy thoughts. "Heather, Paul is on his way to take you to the dance in his truck. The temperature keeps dropping, and it is getting dangerously slippery out there. He should be here in about a half an hour, so hurry and get ready. Remember, I want to take some pictures of you before we leave. I want to show everyone just how lovely you are!"

Heather spies her reflection in the antique oval mirror. She is wearing an ankle-length emerald green velvet dress that falls gently in luxurious folds over her slim hips. She chose the dress because it reminded her of the color of her father's eyes. On her feet are the soft black leather slippers that she and her mom had searched for and finally found after an entire day at the mall. Her thick shoulder-length coppery hair is pulled back into a French braid and intertwined with a green velvet ribbon. Hanging from her neck is the gold locket that her father gave her that last Christmas. Heather touches the locket lovingly and begins to think of him again.

"Oh, Dad," she whispered to herself, "tonight is such a special night for me. How I wish you were here!"

2

CHAPTER TWO

Heather and Jamie

TONIGHT IS A VERY SPECIAL night for Heather because she is going to her first formal dance at the high school. The best part, of course, is that she is going to meet Jamie Schuster there. Her whole face lights up when she thinks about Jamie. Shy, soft-spoken Jamie, with his blue eyes that are fringed by soft brown lashes. Jamie, who has won her young heart with his sweet and gentle ways.

❈

THIS FRIENDSHIP STARTED one morning in early October when Heather was kneeling down trying to find something in the bottom of her locker. She just happened to look up and found herself staring up into a pair of deep blue eyes that were staring right into hers. "Hi," he said. "I was just wondering if you'd like to go for a soda with me this afternoon, right after soccer practice?"

Heather, who was ordinarily a very serious and practical young lady, had to make herself calm down before she could even mouth the words, "That sounds cool, Jamie."

"Great," he replied. "Can you meet me at the soccer field about three thirty?"

Heather swallowed and answered, "Sure."

After he left, Heather had to pinch herself to believe that this had really happened.

It turned out to be a very long day for Heather. Every time she tried to concentrate on something, Jamie's blue eyes would appear in her mind, causing her to become very distracted. She couldn't wait for lunch so that she could share her exciting news with her best friends, Rebecca and Julie.

When the three girls finally sat together at their favorite table in the corner of the cafeteria, Heather blurted out her news. Rebecca and Julie were astonished and happy for her. Of course, they knew that Heather had harbored a secret crush on Jamie for a long time now, but they were not aware that he felt the same way.

"That is just unbelievable," stated Rebecca as she squeezed Heather's hand. Julie, the most emotional one of all of them, was giggling and squirming in her chair. "That is sooo cool, Heather," she exclaimed. "Who would have ever imagined!"

When lunch was over and they were on their way back to class, they made Heather promise to tell them everything that happened that afternoon.

"And we mean everything!" whispered Julie as she ran down the hall.

That afternoon, the weather had turned bitterly cold; and Heather had to really bundle up to walk over to the Soccer Field but when Jamie walked over to her after the practice, Heather didn't know if she was jittery from the cold or from nerves.

Shyly they walked down Main Street toward Angie's Pizza Shop, which was located in the center of town about four or five blocks from the school. This was the place that everyone hung around after school. All the tables appeared to be taken, but fortunately, there was one booth left in the corner next to the jukebox.

The shop was warm and the air fragrant with the smells of basil and oregano. They both ordered a hot chocolate. As they were waiting for their drinks, their eyes accidentally met over the table, and then something magical happened. All of a sudden, it seemed as if they had known each other for ages. Neither of them could stop talking. Sometimes they would literally trip over each other's words.

They shared the same views on so many subjects, and they both loved mushroom pizza, The Beatles, Eric Clapton ice hockey, and skiing. It was as if they had known each other forever.

As the autumn days passed, Heather and Jamie became good friends, as well as soul mates. Several evenings a week, Jamie would drop by and help Heather with her math homework, since he was a senior majoring in math and science. Her younger brother, Jonathon, also looked forward to Jamie's visits because he always gave him special soccer pointers.

Heather and Jamie had very busy schedules. He was captain of the soccer team, as well as a member of the French and math club. He also assisted the head coach in teaching soccer to the kids at the middle school. She, in turn, belonged to the school newspaper and the Spanish club and assisted her mother whenever Sara volunteered to serve meals at the church for the homeless or needy.

Another important part of Heather's life was her service to the elderly. Every Wednesday afternoon, Heather would walk down to Peaceful Gardens. She would serve cookies and tea to the residents and sometimes play the piano for them. The residents loved to get together and sing old songs. Heather enjoyed doing this and was surprised when Jamie volunteered to go with her one day. Afterward, they talked for a long time about social issues; the sick and the elderly and people who were less fortunate than themselves.

The posters for the Westford High School Winter Prom went up the first part of November. Heather looked forward to going to the dance with Jamie. She had yet to attend a formal dance at the school. The day that Jamie did ask her to go with him, Heather ran home so fast to tell her mother that she left her boots at school. However, her feet barely touched the ground, so she didn't feel the cold at all!

CHAPTER THREE

Sara

HEATHER AND HER PARENTS, CHARLIE and Sara, moved to Vermont when she was just a baby. They moved there from Connecticut after Charlie finished his residency at St. Raphael's Hospital in New Haven, Connecticut. Heather's parents had actually met in the emergency room of the hospital two years before when Sara had brought in an injured student.

Sara had been teaching fifth grade at the middle school in Chester, Connecticut. This was a dream come true for Sara. Ever since she was a little girl, she had wanted to teach. Her family lived in Old Saybrook, Connecticut, and so it was easy for her to be home with her family on the weekends. More than anything, however, she loved being in the classroom with her students.

On this particular day, she had stayed after school to coach the girls' soccer team. During one of the plays, a student tripped and came down hard on her left knee. The student, whose name was Barbara, cried out in pain and was not able to move her leg. The compassionate young Sara, instead of waiting for an ambulance, impulsively piled Barbara and several of her concerned teammates into the back of her station wagon and then drove like the wind to

St. Raphael's Hospital. Upon arriving, Sara called Barbara's parents, who were very concerned, of course, and grateful and told Sara that they would be right over.

Dr. Charles Burbank was on duty in the emergency room that particular evening. He was tall and lean, with curly hair that framed his face like a soft copper-colored cap. He also had the most amazing, intense green eyes that appeared to look right through you whenever he talked to you. Dr. Burbank was kind and understanding, and also very concerned about Barbara's leg. Through it all, however, he managed to joke and laugh with the girls, and even asked if they were sisters. His gentle hands examined Barbara's leg and knee very carefully, and then he ordered X-rays. A nurse appeared and helped to get Barbara situated in a wheelchair, and off they went.

Sara could not help but notice that all the while Dr. Burbank was examining Barbara's leg, his eyes seemed to be seeking out her eyes, and she could feel herself blushing and getting a little flustered. She was almost relieved when he left to look at the X-rays with the Orthopedic doctor.

Well, Barbara and her parents and Sara and the rest of the troops all left the hospital in good spirits that night. As it turned out, nothing was broken, only bruised. Barbara had to stay off the leg for a least a week and was instructed not to play soccer for at least three weeks. On the way home, Sara treated all the girls to ice cream.

That night Sara went to bed, exhausted but relieved. Something else happened to Sara that night; just before she drifted off to sleep, she saw a pair of intense green eyes that seemed to wink at her.

Several days later, Sara received a call from young Dr. Charles Burbank. "Hi, Sara," he said. "I got your phone number from the registration desk at the hospital. I hope that you don't mind my calling you. I called for two reasons: one to inquire about the young lady with the injured leg, and the other is to ask you if you would consider going out to dinner with me this weekend."

Sara was very surprised, but also pleased. She smiled to herself and told Charlie that her student, Barbara was coming along just fine and that she would be happy to meet him for dinner on the weekend.

This way, she thought to herself, *if he is unbearable or boring, I can easily excuse myself with a headache and leave.*

Of course, Dr. Charles Burbank was not unbearable or boring, and he and Sara found an understanding and warmth in each other that they had both been searching for. It was the beginning of a wonderful relationship that one year later found them at the altar of Christ's Episcopal Church in Old Saybrook, Connecticut.

CHAPTER FOUR

Elizabeth and Sara

SARA, HEATHERS'S MOTHER WAS BORN in Old Saybrook, Connecticut to Elizabeth and First Lieutenant John Canastro. The family moved around quite a bit, because Sara and Elizabeth would usually go wherever John was stationed. However, when John was called to Vietnam, Elizabeth and Sara moved back to Old Saybrook, where Elizabeth's parents lived. Christian and Sally were getting on in years but were able to help Elizabeth with caring for her little girl.

They helped comfort both Elizabeth and Sara when they were told about John's death. Sara was only six years old when this occurred. John had been mortally wounded in the city of Hue, South Vietnam.

It took Sara a long time to come to the realization that her father, whom she *adored would never come home again.* Elizabeth mourned for herself and for her daughter and for all the other families who lost loved ones during this cruel war.

At this time in her life Elizabeth worked part-time at a local business as a bookkeeper. She, however, coming from good Irish roots, was a survivor. She immediately got a manager's position at a local business and vowed to support herself and her daughter as well as she possibly could. However, God did send her a helper in the form of her brother.

When the war ended, Aaron, who had also been serving in Vietnam, came to live with them. He took the little apartment in the back of the large Cape that Heather's parents had purchased right before John died. Aaron had planned to stay there for only a short while, but as time went by, Elizabeth and Sara began to depend on him more and more. They encouraged him to remain with them and so Aaron stayed.

Aaron had gone to culinary school before the war started, and he took a job with a local restaurant, which he eventually purchased. He spent a lot of time at the restaurant but somehow managed to attend all of Sara's school events with her mother. He was a wonderful uncle to the little girl, and she came to think of him almost as a father.

Even though Aaron was always cheerful and joked around a lot with Sara and her mother, there was a sad, melancholy look in his eyes sometimes. Sara wondered what caused that pained look to come into her uncle's eyes.

She asked her mother about it. "Mom, sometimes in the evening, when I knock at his door, he is just sitting in his chair staring into the fireplace with a sad look on his face." Elizabeth looked down at her ten-year-old daughter and answered, "I know what you're talking about, Heather. *And over the years, I have also noticed that sometimes, when he hears a certain song, or even a certain phrase, it is almost as if a shadow passes over him and he loses his concentration. I think that it must have something to do with the war, because he was never like that before he went to Viet Nam. Remember, Sara, that no matter who we are or what we think, war will always leave us a little damaged."*

Aaron was a marvelous chef and was always concocting something new in the kitchen. Actually, he taught Sara almost everything she knew about cooking. This was a great relief to Elizabeth since she herself was not fond of dabbling in the kitchen.

Aaron contributed to the upkeep of the house and started a

college fund for Sara, so that when the time came, she was able to attend the school of her choice. He never married, although he was engaged once. He was a busy man with a wonderful sense of humor, and he seemed to be content with the company of his sister and her only child.

CHAPTER FIVE

Charlie

*C*HARLIE, HEATHER'S FATHER ON THE other hand, *grew up in a big farmhouse in Avon, Connecticut. He was the younger of two brothers and a very welcome addition to the family. His father, Stanford Burbank, was an extremely successful cardiologist in the Hartford area. His mother, Dr. Anita Burbank, was a psychologist with a small practice in the area. She kept her practice small by choice because she knew that her husband would not be home as much as she and the children would like him to be, and so she made the choice to be the parent in charge of the home and the children most of the time. Anita enjoyed playing with her children, decorating her home, and entertaining. She also* volunteered a lot of her time to the local Methodist church.

The boys grew up in a house full of love and laughter. Anita went into labor for Charlie two weeks early. She would always remember that eventful night because her labor pains started right in the middle of a blinding snowstorm. Slowly she and Stanford made their way through the snow to the car. It was difficult to see and very slippery.

The roads were terrible, and the big Buick kept skidding and sliding on the road.

Anita recalls praying intensely with her eyes shut. She prayed for herself and the unborn child within her. She prayed for her husband, with his strained face, who smiled at her now and then but kept his eyes on the road ahead of him. She prayed for her parents, who were at home taking care of John; and then right in the middle of one of her prayers, a voice softly spoke to her and said, "Don't worry, Anita. Everything is going to be alright." Anita sat up with a start and looked around her. Again, the voice seemed to whisper to her, "Everything is going to be all right. The plans for this child are for good." Then calmness seemed to settle around her. It enveloped her like soft cotton and gave her a feeling of peace and tranquility that was different than she had never known before. She came to the conclusion that perhaps an angel or some heavenly being had just talked to her because she could not believe that here she was, with strong labor pains, traveling in a car in an ice storm, and feeling like this. She turned and smiled at Stanford, who also seemed to be smiling at her as the car skidded into the hospital parking lot.

That feeling of calmness seemed to stay with Anita all through the delivery. She felt safe and secure and totally at peace.

Charlie was born at 3:00 AM without any complications, and the funny thing about him was that he never cried. He just nursed peacefully and fell asleep.

Later on in life, when Anita was going through stressful or difficult times, that wonderful feeling of peace would come again, and she would always associate it with the presence of angels. She was a wise woman.

After high school, both boys attended the University of Connecticut, but chose very different paths. John pursued Journalism, and Charlie pursued Medicine.

John did very well in his writing career and landed a job with a very popular magazine. He was constantly traveling all over the world and enjoyed every bit of it. Anita and Stanford wished that he would settle down and have a family, but John was not having any part of it. He was seldom home or ever in one place long enough to develop a serious relationship.

You can imagine how overjoyed they were when Charlie brought

Sara home for dinner one evening. They were delighted with her and hoped with all their heart that she was the one for Charlie.

When the young couple began to make wedding plans, Anita thought that surely her heart would burst with joy!

CHAPTER SIX

Charlie and Sara

THE WEDDING WAS TO BE held at the Episcopal Church on Main Street in Old Saybrook. It was an elegant and beautiful church, built entirely of gray stone and covered with a slate roof.

Elizabeth and Aaron were also very happy for Charlie and Sara. They enjoyed Charlies' good humor and laughter. They felt that he was good for Sara, since she seemed to be very serious a lot of the time. All of Sara's family were very active in the community and knew both the church pastors quite well.

The location did not prove to be a problem with Charlie's parents because they had spent numerous summers on the Old Saybrook seashore and had many friends in the area.

It was a joyful yet solemn candlelight ceremony. Sara looked enchanting in her cream-colored gown as she walked down the isle on her uncle's arm. The love that Charlie had for her was visible in his very being as he took her arm and they stepped up to the altar. The young couple had chosen their own verses to recite to each other.

Sara had chosen from the book of Ruth. She whispered, "Where you go, Charlie, I will go, and where you lodge, I will lodge. Your people shall be my people, and your God, my God."[1]

He, in turn, chose to read from the book of Proverbs. "He that finds a wife finds a good thing and obtains favor from the Lord. Sara, by wisdom our house will be built and by understanding, it will be established. And by knowledge the rooms will be filled with all precious and pleasant riches."[2]

Just before the young couple repeated their vows, a hushed silence fell over the church, and the presence of divine love could be felt in the air. It was as if the very stones wanted to sing for joy! Surely, the angels in heaven were singing as well.

Charlie had only one more year at St. Raphael's Hospital order to finish up his residency. Unlike his father, Charlie had chosen to go into Family Medicine and had never regretted it.

Charlie and Sara decided to rent a small condo in Madison, Connecticut. This would be an easy communicate for both of them.

Heather was born one year later on the first day of May. What a joyful day that was for both families. A little girl was very welcome and they named her Heather. Both Charlie and Sara were thrilled with this tiny, new life and vowed to everything within their power to give her a wonderful and loving childhood.

---

[1] The Topical Chain Study Bible
[2] The Topical Chain Study Bible (Reference)
 New American Standard esidency.

CHAPTER SEVEN

Life in Vermont

H EATHER, PERHAPS, WAS ONE OF the reasons that they decided to pack up all their belongings and move to Vermont. It was a decision that they would never regret.

Charlie had learned about a position in Westford, Vermont, from his friend and former college roommate, Dr. Joshua Cohen.

Joshua was practicing in Burlington, Vermont, and looked forward to having Charlie close by again. The position was challenging because Charlie would be the only full-time physician at a place called the North Mountain Clinic.

The small staff consisted of a physician's assistant, another part-time MD, Joshua from Burlington and two part time nurses.

The Burbank family went house hunting about three months before they moved. It was the middle of September, and there was a definite chill in the air.

Heather was all bundled up in a pink snowsuit. Her cheeks were apple red, and her green eyes sparkled. Her parents pushed her around the town in her stroller as they followed the realtor from one house to the other. Charlie wanted to live in close proximity to the clinic.

Finally, they settled upon a charming old Victorian with a

wraparound porch. In later years, Heather would have delightful tea parties with her dolls and teddy bears on that lovely porch.

The house had a huge fireplace in the front room and a loud, scary oil burner in the basement. The large backyard was enclosed by a weathered gray wooden fence that was covered with bittersweet and tiny wild roses. The kitchen and the bathrooms had to be renovated, but Charlie was pretty handy; and he felt that with the right tools and a little help, anything could be accomplished.

The house was located on Bridge Street, and rightly so, since there was an antique covered bridge on one end of the road that led off into the mountains. The location was great because it was situated right off of Main Street, only about a mile's walking distance from the clinic.

THE CLINIC ITSELF was a renovated rambling farmhouse with an attached barn. The main house served as the actual clinic while the barn served as a storage place for everything conceivable.

In the main house, there were two tiny offices, a waiting room, two small examining rooms, an X-ray cubicle, and a lab cubicle. There was also a bathroom and a small kitchen with a cot in one corner just in case a patient had to spend the night.

In the waiting room, there was an ancient pot bellied stove that stood in the corner. It was great for warming frozen fingers, toes and frosty bottoms. There was a large old-fashioned iron kettle on the stove that was brewing tea at all times. Charlie loved the robust flavor of strong tea. The unique smells of ethyl alcohol, strong tea, and burning wood permeated the clinic.

These smells would remain locked in Heather's brain for the rest of her life, especially the fragrance of fresh-brewed tea because it reminded her instantly of her father.

Joshua would come in from Burlington two days a week to assist Charlie at the clinic. Whenever Joshua was in town, he would eat with Heather's family because he lived alone in the city, and Sara insisted that he have a home-cooked meal.

Friendly and good-natured. Heather looked forward to the visits from Dr. Cohen. On occasion, he and Charlie would reminisce about their college days, and sometimes they would laugh so hard that tears would run down their cheeks.

The best part, however, was when Joshua and Charlie decided to have a football game in the yard. Everybody would get to join in and roll all over the lawn and laugh even harder. Sometimes the neighbors would even join in.

Heather could remember those musky fall evenings when there was a chill in the air and the vibrant colors of the trees were fading. Now in the mornings, there was always a promise of snow on the horizon.

The little clinic all of a sudden became very busy, and Joshua attributed this to Charlie's presence and his concern and respect for the people of the area. To Charlie, each patient was unique and special. He showed great compassion for each and every person. He treated the elderly and the infirm with patience and understanding and delivered babies for some of the town's poorest.

He was also involved in the diagnosis and treatment of the area's small population of HIV patients. Many times, he paid for their medication out of his own pocket because it was so expensive.

The people in the town grew to love and respect Charlie Burbank, and even the "old-timers" called on him when they had a problem., On several occassions, Doc Charlie, as they came to call him, had to take the old Roadrunner that belonged to the clinic and make a house call. Sometimes this took him high into the mountains to treat an old-timer who had the Flu or had fallen out of a tree or off a ladder and banged himself up. Several days later, after one of these visits, there would appear on their doorstep some sort of token, such as a sack of potatoes, a couple of dozens of wood for their fireplace. One time someone even left a cage with three live, cackling hens.

CHAPTER EIGHT

Jonathon

WHEN HEATHER WAS FOUR YEARS old and finishing up her preschool year when her parents joyously informed her that she was going to have a baby brother or sister soon. Well, Heather became very excited and very, very impatient! She could not believe that she had to wait such a long time for this wonderful event to take place.

⟷⟷

HEATHER STARTED SCHOOL in September at the Westford Primer, as it was called in the town. It housed grades first through fourth, with only about fifteen children to each classroom. She made friends right away with two girls who were to become her soul mates and companions for life. One was named Rebecca, and the other was named Julie.

Julie Connelly was a tiny, petite child with blonde ringlets that fell in unruly bundles all over her face. She was a rather aggressive little girl with an exuberant personality that sometimes got her into trouble. Her parents lived right across the street from the town green and about five blocks from Heather's house. Julie's father, Douglas, was the Rector of St. James Episcopal Church. Her mother, Mary

Catharine, became very friendly with Sara; and Douglas and Charlie also got on well, so the girls were together quite often, which was just fine with them.

Rebecca, Heather's other companion, lived in a large modern ranch house close to the school. She was the quietest of all three, but never failed to join in their laughter when something struck them as really funny. She was blessed with long thick black hair and large dark eyes. Her complexion was a light olive color, and this gave her a classic Mediterranean beauty.

As the girls grew older and were able to walk to school together, they would take turns stopping at each other's house after school.

Rebecca's mother, Heather thought, was the best baker in the world. On cold winter nights, Elaine would make delicious cookies and pastries to have with cups of hot, steamy tea or chocolate for the girls.

ON SEVERAL OCCASIONS, Heather was invited to the special Friday-evening Sabbath dinner at Rebecca's house. She thought that perhaps the rest of the world was really missing something by not sharing in this old and wonderful tradition.

CHAPTER NINE

Charlie

CHARLIE BURBANK WAS A COMPASSIONATE and excellent physician, but he also took his role as a father very seriously. He always tried to make time to spend with his children, especially in the evening. His name of endearment for Heather was angel, and he told her many times that as she grew older, she looked more and more like an enchanting angel.

Heather loved it when they spent time together. Sometimes, after dinner, when Charlie was not at the clinic, she would sit on his lap on the rocker in front of the fireplace. As the flames crackled and the cold wind blew outside, Charlie would talk to Heather about angels.

"Celestial beings or angels," Charlie would say, "are all around us, but very few of us are aware of them." He seemed to know a lot about angels.

"Do you know, Heather, that angels are messengers from God? They always have a mission, and sometimes, when things seem really bad, they just come around to let you know that God has not forgotten you. One thing for sure," he would say, "when you are going through some difficult times, you can always call on the angels to help you and protect you. Sometimes, they will even talk to you, but you have to be very still and listen very carefully and believe."

"Sometimes they will talk to you in your sleep, or even when you are praying. They may not always make things turn out the way that you want them to, but they surely always make things turn out for the best for everyone, even though you may not realize it at the time. Sometimes it may take us a while to understand what God is doing but eventually we will realize and delight in what has occurred." Charlie would then quote from the ninety-first psalm, "'And He will give His angels charge over you to guide you in all your ways. They will bear you up in their hands, lest you strike your foot against a stone.'"

"What do they look like, Dad?" she would ask. "Have you ever seen one?" Charlie would reply, "Oh, Heather, they come in all different sizes, dressed in different clothes. Sometimes they are walking right beside you in the mall or in town. Perhaps, even when you are sitting at a restaurant, they may be sitting at the next table or booth. One thing for sure, Heather, if you watch and listen, you will always know when there is an angel nearby."

Heather loved to hear about the angels, and she wondered why her daddy knew so much about them.

CHAPTER TEN

Jonathon

JONATHON MATTHEW BURBANK WAS BORN on November 12, right before Thanksgiving, and what a joyous event it was! The house smelled of flowers and baby powder and pumpkin pie.

Heather was fascinated by this adorable, moving creature. She loved to help her mother with him and was always the first to tell Sara if Jonathon was fussy or wet or hungry.

As Jonathon grew, Heather enjoyed him more and more. When he started walking, she would take him outside in the front yard and play ball with him and on occasion, she would take him with her to visit her friends. Julie had a little sister who was one year older than Jonathon, and the two little ones would crawl around on the floor playing with their toys and balls.

Sara was very aware of all the help that Heather was to her, and she went out of her way to praise and thank Heather whenever she did something special. She also tried to put time aside to spend with Heather without the baby. One of their favorite things to do together was to spend the entire day shopping at the Burlington Mall. Other days, they would just go out for a quiet lunch together and share girl talk. Heather loved those special times with her mother, and as she grew older, she and Sara remained close. They were good friends, as well as mother and daughter.

Time passed for the Burbank family. Sara began to substitute at Heather's school, and on those particular days, Jonathon would stay with Mrs. McCarthy, a wonderful, nurturing woman that they had found through the church. She was a widow with no children of her own. Mrs. McCarthy was also a great cook, and sometimes she would help Sara by preparing dinner for all of the family. It did not take long for the Burbank family to adopt her as one of their own.

CHAPTER ELEVEN

Adventures

THE NORTHERN MOUNTAIN CLINIC CONTINUED to grow, and there was talk in the town about expansion, but Charlie said that this would take time and planning. When Heather turned eight years old, she and Julie and Rebecca began to take ski lessons. Through many tumbles and bumps and bruises, they all eventually learned to ski, and to do it well. Julie was by far the most daring, and both Rebecca and Heather told her that one day, she was going to be sorry. As it was, she did run into a tree one time when she was about twelve years old and had to be carried down the hill on the clinic sled. She suffered a mild concussion, according to Dr. Burbank, but that didn't stop her. One week later, she was back on the slopes again. However, Heather and Julie would never let her forget that incident!

As the girls grew older and became more proficient, they were allowed to pack a picnic lunch and spend the entire day on the slopes. These were laughter-filled, cold, sunshiny days, and the girls would always cherish those memories.

The best part of skiing all day was coming home. Heather loved coming home in the late afternoon to a cozy home with the kettle whistling on the stove. Even if Sara was still at school, Mrs. McCarthy was always there with soup and some sort of cookie that she had baked.

Responsibilities in the Burbank household were shared by all. Of course, Jonathon was still too young to be really involved, but Heather had quite an agenda. She was in charge of keeping an eye on the supplies of paper goods in the house. These included paper towels, napkins, toilet paper, and paper plates and cups. She was also responsible for loading the dishwasher at night and starting it.

Outside of the home, she was also very busy. On Wednesday nights, she had piano lessons with the "Good" sisters, as they called themselves.

They were two characters right out of a Victorian novel. They wore their hair up in little buns on top of their heads and always dressed in long dresses with lovely old fashioned pinafores around their waists. They also always carried little lace handkerchiefs in their pockets.

Their names were Jenny and Emily, and they gave music lessons to most of the children in Westford. Neither sister had ever married, so they liked to think of the children as part of their family. They were well known for their elegant Christmas parties, to which both students and parents were invited.

On Thursday evenings, Heather accompanied Sara and Mary Catharine and Julie to the Episcopal church, where they assisted in the soup kitchen and served meals once a week. Sometimes Mrs. Stein, Rebecca's mom, would also come, and the girls looked forward to this because it gave them all another opportunity to chat.

Heather's summers also bustled with activity. She always spent the first two weeks of July with Grandpa and Grandma Burbank at their farm in Avon, Connecticut. Heather loved to visit the stables and brush the horses. She became an accomplished equestrian there and also mastered the difficult task of milking a cow. Those were fun filled summers, and the smell of Grandma Anita's homemade blueberry pies (with the blueberries that Heather had picked) baking in the oven was enough to make everyone's mouth water.

The first two weeks of August were spent with Grandma Elizabeth and Uncle Aaron. Grandma Elizabeth loved the seashore, and she and Heather took long walks by the ocean and collected lovely smooth stones polished by the waves and strange luminescent-colored shells. Heather kept a large glass jar in her room and filled it with all her treasures from the sea.

When Uncle Aaron was not working at the restaurant, he would be digging around in his garden, and he loved to share all his gardening tips with Heather. He grew all his own vegetables and then, of course, concocted the most delicious meals from his harvest. Friends were always invited for dinner, and there were always numerous toasts, wine, and laughter. Since Uncle Aaron was a chef, a meal was not just a meal, but a thing of flavor and beauty to be enjoyed for hours. Many times, Heather would be sleepy and ready for bed even before dessert was served.

CHAPTER TWELVE

Thanksgiving

JOSHUA, NOW HAD A VERY good "friend"; and on occasion, she would accompany him when he visited the Burbanks. Everyone enjoyed themselves immensely when Joshua and Paige came over. Charlie would open up a bottle of wine, and before dinner, there would always be cheese and crackers in front of the fireplace, with Mozart playing in the background. Heather and Jonathon never felt left out because there would always be sparkling apple or grape juice for their enjoyment. The children felt very grown up when they were allowed to partake in these festivities.

The holidays came and brought with them snow and visitors and more love than children could hold in their heart. Heather remembered one particular Thanksgiving. It was the one that centered around a deer.

Charlie and Joshua had actually gone deer hunting, and Joshua had "bagged" a deer. Granpa and Grandma Burbank had come for dinner and brought Uncle John, Charlie's brother. Uncle John did not come very often since he was always flying all over the world for a story.

The deer was prepared and served, along with the turkey, on

Thanksgiving Day. Heather felt very sorry for the creature and confided this to Grandma Anita. "Oh, Grandma, I don't think that I can possibly eat any part of that poor deer." Grandma understood and told Heather that it was all right to just enjoy the turkey.

Uncle John began to tell stories about his "deer-hunting days," and Heather and Jonathon were amazed and hypnotized with all his adventures. Grandpa Burbank just laughed and said, "John, John, you truly know how to tell a good yarn!"

Despite the presence of the deer at the table, the dinner was outstanding and delicious. There were homemade rolls, pies, and cookies. Jonathon fell asleep in his chair, and Heather could hardly move when she excused herself from the table.

Afterward, they all sat around in the big front room with the fire crackling and listened to Vivaldi on the stereo. Grandpa fell asleep in the big leather chair near the fireplace, and Charlie put his head in Sara's lap and snoozed on the couch. Baby Jonathon curled up with his blanket on the little loveseat, while their dog, Penny, nuzzled his ear. Heather snuggled up near Grandma in the den, where, together, they watched the snow come down. Heather shared stories of her friends and school events and just life in general with her grandmother. Grandma Burbank was always very interested in everything that Heather said or did and gave her, her undivided attention.

The house was cozy and warm and smelled of cinnamon and turkey and brown sugar. Heather felt so warm and good inside. She wondered if angels ever had special celebrations like this.

CHAPTER THIRTEEN

Mysterious

ONE VERY HOT SUMMER, TOWARD the end of August or the beginning of September, when Heather was about twelve years old, she began to notice some subtle changes in her father. She couldn't quite put her finger on it, but she knew that Charlie was acting differently somehow.

Charlie's normal routine after he came home for lunch every day was to take a short nap, because the clinic was closed from 12:00 to 2:00 PM, unless there was an emergency, of course. After his nap, he would awaken refreshed and ready to go back to the work that he loved so dearly. Charlie spent long hours at the clinic and sometimes did not get home until 7:00 or 8:00 PM.

Lately, however, Heather noticed that her father was just leaving the house when she arrived home from school at three or three thirty in the afternoon. She asked her mother about it, and Sara replied, "Oh, hon, your dad is very worn out lately, and it's gotten rather difficult to wake him up from his nap. We're both hoping that he'll get more help when the winter season hits."

Heather also observed that her dad had stopped running in the morning, and when he did, it was for shorter periods of time. She had always been able to gauge how much time she had in which to eat her breakfast, get dressed, and get ready for school according to the time it took Charlie to run his three miles around the town. Now it seemed as if he was back before Heather had even started eating breakfast.

She also discovered that her father would fall asleep many evenings in the old rocker by the fire, because she could hear Sara trying to wake him to come to bed.

Thes events went on for about four months until Joshua began to get really worried and insisted that Charlie go to the hospital in Burlington and have some tests.

"Listen, Charlie, you and I have been friends for a long time, and I would be dishonest if I didn't admit to you that Sara and I are both getting a little concerned."

"Come on, Joshua," Charlie replied. "It's just a virus. I'll start eating better. Sara will put me on a strict health food diet. Lots of tofu, yogurt, and no red meat. I'll come out of this slump. Look, I'm feeling stronger already," he said as he ran and picked up Jonathon and threw him over his shoulders.

Joshua, however, would not take no for an answer, and the appointments were made.

Heather remembered that day very well. It was embedded in her memory and could never be erased.

It was a Friday morning during the first week of December. It was cold and blustery, with the temperature hovering around the middle teens. That morning, everyone was a little tense and anxious. She remembered the look on her mother's face. Somehow Heather could not remember her mother ever having looked that forlorn or worried.

Heather did not want to go to school, but Sara insisted, saying, "Heather, Mary Catherine and I are going to have lunch together and do a little shopping for Christmas. We will all try to keep our spirits up and pray for the best. I will be here waiting for you when you come home. Your father and Joshua promise to call us as soon as they know anything."

CHAPTER FOURTEEN

Waiting

I T WAS VERY DIFFICULT FOR Heather to concentrate that entire day. Her friends Julie and Rebecca tried to reassure her at lunchtime, but still and all, it was a long day for her. When school was over Heather ran home as fast as she could to hear the news.

As soon as she walked in the door, she knew that something was wrong. Her mother was sitting in the kitchen all by herself. She seemed very agitated and upset. She told Heather that there had been no telephone call yet!

Heather noticed that her mother could not sit still. She got up from the table and began walking aimlessly from room to room with a faraway look in her eyes. It was as if she had withdrawn into herself. Heather had never seen her mother in such a state before. She wondered where Jonathon was.

Softly, so as not to worry Sara, she went from room to room, calling, "Jonathon, Jonathon, where are you?" Finally, she heard his voice from the small bedroom that was located in the back of the house. Her parents did not like them to go in there because the room had no heat in it and it was always very cold and drafty.

Jonathon was sitting on the bed sharing his peanut butter and jelly sandwich with Penny, their old shepherd, who was enjoying every bite. He still had his hat and coat on. When he saw Heather, he jumped off the bed and spilled his glass of milk. "Where did Mom go?," he asked Heather as he tried to sop up the milk with his wooly hat. "She said that she would be right back and she hasn't returned."

"What a mess!" thought Heather to herself. She took Jonathon by his hand and led him into the little bathroom next to the kitchen. She asked him to wash his face and hands and then coaxed him into the Study where she told him that he could watch his favorite Movie on CD. Penny, the dog followed him around looking for more handouts. When Jonathon seemed occupied, Heather left the room and then picked up a broom and some paper towels and went into the back room to clean up the milk. As she was coming out of the room, she thought that she could hear someone crying. Slowly she followed the sounds up the stairs to her parents' bedroom. Sara was sitting on the edge of the bed looking at the phone on the side table with tears in her lovely eyes.

Heather walked over to her mother and gently took her hand. Finally, Sara's sobs subsided. She looked up at her daughter and then hugged her very tightly. Without saying a word, she rose from the chair; walked into the bathroom, where she washed her face; and then slowly left the room and walked down the stairs. In the living room, she went about starting a fire in the fireplace. Sara was acting as if she was in a trance.

Heather prepared grilled cheese sandwiches and tomato soup for dinner. She and her mother and Jonathon ate dinner by themselves that evening in front of the fire. It was as if Sara needed the warmth near her body.

The great regulator clock in the hallway chimed the half hour, and Heather noticed that it was already seven thirty.

Sara told Jonathon that it was his bedtime and Jonathan did not even object. He slowly climbed the stairs with a mournful face. It was as if a spirit of sadness had come over all of them.

Sara followed him up the stairs and into his room. After Jonathon had brushed his teeth and put on his pajamas, she sat on Jonathon's bed. They said prayers together and they prayed especially for Charlie and then she tucked him into bed.

Just then, the telephone rang. It seemed to awaken Sara from her reverie, and she ran to her bedroom to answer it. It was Joshua, just telling her that they were on their way home. "He would not say anything else," she told Heather.

Heather was loading the dishwasher when Sara walked into the kitchen.

"Come and sit by me near the fire, Heather." Heather did as her mother asked and followed her into the living room and sat on the large hassock next to her mother's chair.

"Heather," Sara said, "no matter what happens, even if we don't understand it, remember that we have to take care of each other and remain a family. I know that your father has talked to you a great deal about faith in God and love. I know that he has talked to you about angels, and although I may not agree with everything he believes, I know that we both believe that when things do not work out the way we want them to, we have to trust the Lord even when we don't feel like it or understand what is happening."

She also talked to her about the great love that she and Charlie had for each other and for their children. "The strongest thing we can have for each other is love, for love overcomes everything," Sara said.

Outside, it was beginning to snow and little white flakes could be seen at the windows. Heather and her mother had some hot chocolate, and then they walked up the to her room.

Together they prayed for Charlie and Joshua and asked God to bring them home safely.

Heather tossed and turned for a long time that night, but she knew that her father and Charlie had come home because she heard their voices just before she slipped into a restless slumber.

CHAPTER FIFTEEN

Changes

THE NEXT DAY WAS SATURDAY, and Heather woke with a start. She could hear voices and clatter coming from downstairs. She pulled on her fleece robe and furry slippers and pattered down.

Jonathon was sitting at the kitchen table eating French toast, and Charlie was singing as he fried bacon on the stove. Sara was unloading the dishwasher. Joshua had left earlier to open up the clinic.

"Hi, angel," Charlie said to Heather and smiled. Everything seemed so normal. Only Sara's eyes showed traces of sadness when she looked at her daughter.

It had started to snow again, and Charlie suggested that they all go outside and have a snowball fight after breakfast. Jonathon loved snowball fights.

They all piled outside and were soon joined by their neighbors, the Whitmans and their son Paul. Paul had just arrived here from Tennessee and had taken a position as the seventh-grade math teacher at the junior high school.

They tussled all over the yard and laughed and rolled around in the snow. Heather's face hurt from the cold and from laughing so much.

In the afternoon, Heather, Rebecca and Julie went ice skating at the college rink. Then Charlie, Sara, Jonathon, Paige, and Joshua came and picked them up and took them to Angie's Pizza Shop for dinner. It was a great day. Heather wondered if angels ate pizza. She also wondered if perhaps the young couple sitting in the booth across the room were angels, because now and then, Heather would look up and catch the girl's eye. Each time this happened, she would experience a strange tingling sensation from the tips of her toes to the top of her head.

The next day was Sunday, and all of them attended the ten o'clock service at St. James. Everything seemed normal to Heather, and she was just beginning to start her homework at about three in the afternoon when the doorbell rang. It was Douglas and Mary Catharine Connelly. They were accompanied by several other members of the church. Heather thought that perhaps they were part of the prayer group that she had seen praying over people after the services. Charlie and Sara took them into the front room and closed the double doors behind them. Heather could hear them talking quietly for several hours.

CHAPTER SIXTEEN

Bits and Pieces

LIFE BEGAN TO CHANGE IN little bits and pieces. Charlie started to go to work later in the morning, and sometimes when he came home for lunch, he was too tired to return. Joshua and the physician's assistant were at the clinic almost every day now.

Sometimes, late at night, when Heather came downstairs for a glass of milk, she would find her father sitting in front of the fireplace reading the Bible. On several occasions, he called her over, and they would sit together, and he would put his arms around her and just hold her. Sometimes he would talk with her about God and the angels and heaven. On one particular night, he told her that he was going to have to start going to the hospital several times a week for some special treatments. "But don't worry, angel," he told her, "our times are in God's hands, and He knows what He is doing." Heather felt that he had a remarkable faith in God. Somehow, she could not bring herself to trust God as Charlie did.

Heather began to feel very melancholy, and she shared all her fears with Rebecca and Julie. They were always there for her and always willing to listen. Rebecca gave her advice in her own quiet, caring way; and Julie, ever the optimist, was always trying to cheer her up.

Charlie was going for treatments on a regular basis, and after about six months, it appeared that he was going into remission. He seemed to be gaining weight, and some of his old vitality appeared to be seeping back into his bones. He stayed for prayer many times after church, and everyone felt that the prayers had been answered.

Everyone seemed happier. Perhaps Charlie was going to beat this after all.

A year went by and the holiday season was upon them again before they knew it. Heather was invited to spend a weekend in New York with Rebecca and her family. At first, she did not want to go, but Sara encouraged her and gave her a long shopping list.

Rebecca's mother and aunt took the girls shopping all morning, and then to a Broadway play in the afternoon. The next day, Heather had the honor of celebrating the first night of Hanukkah with Rebecca and all of her family from New York. It was a beautiful and joyful occasion. Heather felt such love for all of them. She enjoyed herself a great deal, but in her heart, there was still a little bit of sadness. She wondered if angels lived in New York and if perhaps they had passed some right on the street. She thought that this would be difficult to tell since there were so many people in New York City.

She returned home to find Sara, Jonathon, Joshua, and Paige putting the lights on the big pine tree in front of the house. When they finished and turned on the lights, the tree sparkled and glittered. It was magical in the cold winter night. *I'll bet angels love Christmas trees*, she thought to herself.

The next day, Joshua and Paige went back to Burlington. However, late that afternoon, Joshua called and spoke with Charlie for a long time. Charlie took the phone call in the den and closed the door. When he finally got off the phone, he and Sara went up into their bedroom and stayed there until dusk.

CHAPTER SEVENTEEN

Plans

ONE EVENING, ABOUT TWO DAYS before Christmas, after Jonathon had gone to bed, Charlie called Heather into the family room. He pulled the old hassock next to his chair and asked Heather to sit down.

Lovingly he ran his fingers through her thick coppery locks. "How is my enchanting angel?" he asked. Heather looked up at him and noticed how thin and frail he had become. She did notice, however, that his eyes did not look sad, but almost peaceful. Those peaceful green eyes met Heathers, and he began to talk very quietly.

"Heather," he said, "you know that your mother and I love you very much, and we are also very proud of you. From the day that you and your brother came into this world, your mom and I have adored both of you. You have made life worth living. Please remember that no matter what happens, you will always be my enchanting angel.

"Things are going to be difficult in the days to come, and I want you to promise me that you will help your mother as much as possible. No matter what happens, Heather, remember that I expect you to do well in school and to go on to college. You are a very gifted and talented young lady, and I want you to use your gifts and talents in the best way possible".

"As you get older, angel, you are going to have to make some very difficult choices, but please be aware that for every choice that you make, there is a consequence that will go along with it. Think and pray before you make any decisions. In my heart, I know that God has a wonderful and meaningful life planned for you."

Then Charlie began to talk with her about the angels. He told her that God was preparing a place for him, and he quoted to her from John 14: "'In my father's house are many dwelling places; if it were not so, I would have told you; for I go to prepare a place for you.'"[3]

Heather began to cry and put her arms around him. She whispered to him, "Daddy, please don't go. We love you, and we need you. I don't want you to go to be with the angels. Oh, Daddy, please don't go!"

Silent tears ran down Charlie's face as he held his cherished daughter in his arms. He said, "There is one thing that I want you to remember, Heather, and that is that I will always be with you no matter where you are or what you are doing. All you have to do, Heather, is believe. Just believe, and I will be there for you."

Charlie held her for a long, long time, and all that could be heard in that graceful old Vermont home that night was the ticking of the antique regulator clock and the sound of Heather's sobs.

Early on Christmas Eve day, the Burbanks arrived along with Uncle John; and later in the evening, Grandma Elizabeth and Uncle Aaron drove into the driveway.

All of them attended Christmas Eve Mass together at St. James, but even though they were celebrating the birth of the babe in the manger, they knew in their hearts that soon they would be mourning the loss of one of their own.

---

[3] 1989 NRSV Holy Bible

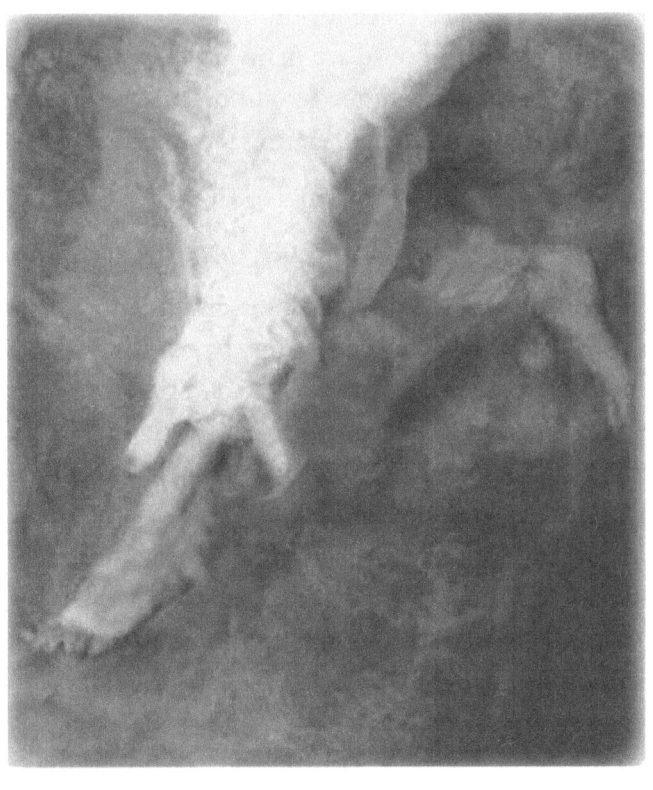

CHAPTER EIGHTEEN

Three Long Days

IN FEBRUARY, CHARLIE SPENT A week in the hospital in Burlington. Heather did not like to visit him there because he was hooked up to all kinds of tubes and machines, and he always seemed very sleepy. Her friends Julie and Rebecca were real troopers, though, and were always waiting for her after these visits with encouraging and comforting words.

Charlie was released from the hospital and came home on a bright Saturday afternoon in late February. Sara stayed by his bedside almost all day long.

Mrs. McCarthy came to the house to prepare the evening meal. This went on for about three days. Heather tried to go to school and to concentrate, but it was extremely hard for her. She wanted to be home with her father.

CHAPTER NINETEEN

Saddness

TUESDAY NIGHT, HEATHER HAD A dream. She saw an angel. No one had to tell her. She knew it was an angel. He was tall and stately. His clothes shone as if made of burnished gold, and there was light all around him. He was looking down, and she could not see his face. When he raised his head and looked at her, she saw that it was her father's face. "No," she cried and sat up in bed.

She opened her eyes and looked around. It was still very dark. She wanted to run to her parents' room. She wanted to shout. She wanted to tell someone, but she could not move. Something was holding her. Something would not let her move. Then suddenly, Heather felt extremely tired, so very, very tired.

She lay back down on her bed and fell into a deep, dreamless sleep.

Sara walked softly into Heather's room at about 6:00 AM. She looked exhausted, with dark circles under her eyes. Slowly she sat on the edge of Heather's bed and shook her gently. "Heather," Sara whispered, "your father died peacefully last night. He told me that he saw the angels and that they had come to carry him home." Heather just stared at her mother. She felt as if there was something broken inside of her and she could not breathe or swallow. She felt as if she were choking. Her breath would not come.

⸙

"Just take little breaths, Heather," Sara whispered. "Just try to relax and take little breaths."

Sara held her in her arms and gently rocked her until Heather could breathe regularly again. Then she kissed her on the forehead and said, "Heather, I'm going downstairs to make you some tea. Stay here and try to relax, and then come on downstairs when you are ready. There are many things that are going to have to be taken care of today, and I know that I am going to need your help. Try to be strong and calm, and God will get us through this time."

After her mother left, Heather got out of bed and slowly began to walk around the room. She could not believe how calm her mother was. She herself felt as if she was living in a dream. She was numb all over, and the worst part was that she could not cry. It was as if all her feelings and emotions had just vanished.

The sermon was given by their good friend and priest Douglas Connelly.

"Charlie Burbank," he said, "was my friend, and so I grieve with all of you. We could say to ourselves, 'Perhaps we should have prayed a little harder, perhaps if we had more faith. Perhaps then Charlie would have stayed with us on this earth.' It is difficult sometimes to understand the mysterious ways of the Lord. However, this I do know, and that is that God has a plan and his ways are higher than our ways, and our lives are truly in his hands. I know that Charlie left us in peace and with a strong belief that he was going home."

"He will be greatly missed, not only by his family and friends, but by all the people of this community. I am sure that he touched all of our lives in one way or another. He had a way of bringing out the best in us. He touched that part of our humanity that is good and honorable and kind. We were privileged to have him with us for this short while. I am quite sure, my friends, that the angels and all the company of heaven are celebrating today because one of their

45

own has come home. So let us not be sad, but instead, let us celebrate with Charlie, and let us keep his spirit alive in this community—his compassion, his generosity, and his love."

Charlie Burbank was buried in the little cemetery that belonged to the parish of St. James Church. It was about three miles out of town, with a little brook running the length of it. Charlie's grave was near the little brook, where the birds sang in the lovely maples and the gurgling sound of the water was almost comforting. It was peaceful there.

When the family arrived home, the house was full of people. The dining room table was covered with a beautiful lace tablecloth on which rested a variety of steaming platters of meats, vegetables, casseroles, and desserts.

Some of Charlie's favorite Mozart pieces were playing in the background, and there were pictures of him on the coffee table. The pictures represented his life: first as a baby, then a boy, then a young man, and then as an adult with his wife and children surrounding him.

Jonathon seemed to be taking all this in stride; however, he did seem to spend most of his time with Uncle John and Uncle Aaron. Sara also appeared to be very busy talking and reminiscing with people, although a couple of times, Heather noticed that there were tears in the corners of her eyes.

In her heart and mind, Heather knew that this was a part of the healing process, but she just could not bring herself to socialize and chat with people. So she slowly made her way to the back porch, where she sat on one of the benches and just thought about her father.

CHAPTER TWENTY

Why God?

"WHY, GOD?" SHE ASKED. "WHY did you have to take my father? What kind of a God are you that you could have allowed this to happen? What good can possibly come from my father's death? If there really are angels, and if You are the great God that the Bible says You you are, then you would bring my father back so that our family would be whole again. How can I believe in you if I am so angry with you? I'll never trust you again!"

Suddenly, she felt a hand on her shoulder. It was her grandmother Elizabeth. Heather looked up at her. Her grandmother's face looked tired and drawn, and yet there was a peace about her eyes that Heather could not understand.

Elizabeth sat down beside her and began to speak. "You know, Heather, when your grandfather died in Vietnam, I was angry and hurt for a long time. Of course, I could not let it get the best of me because I had a little girl. I had to get on with my life. I tried to stay angry with God, but I found that in that state of mind, I could accomplish nothing. Finally, I let Him have my anger and frustration and sadness and I asked him for His help in building a new life, and of course, He did help me in every way possible. I have been blessed in so many ways that sometimes it is overwhelming and humbling." Heather just stared at her grandmother. How could she possibly think that this was blessing? she thought to herself. Slowly Heather got up from the bench and climbed the stairs to her bedroom. Exhausted, she fell on her bed and slept.

CHAPTER TWENTY-ONE

Different Life

SPRING CAME TO THE VERMONT Mountains early that year. Everything was fresh and new and green. The three Burbanks also began to build a new life.

Sara continued to substitute at the grammar school and talked about taking a full-time position. Mrs. McCarthy came over at least three or four times a week. She helped to prepare the evening meal and to be there for Heather and Jonathon when Sara was working. The children seldom came home to an empty house.

The little community of Westford enveloped Sara and her children with support and encouragement and love. Sara could call on any number of people if she was ever in need of anything.

A year went by. The holidays were the worst for Heather. The first year, they went to the farm in Avon to visit Grandma and Grandpa Burbank for Christmas. Charlie's brother, John, was there with a new girlfriend. Her name was Mary, and she and Sara got along very well. The engagement announcement came at the dinner table, and of course, wedding plans were happily discussed.

Heather noticed that a couple of times during the day, Grandma

Anita had to turn her head to hide her tears, and that Grandpa cleared his throat a lot and blew his nose quite often.

Another year came and went. Heather turned fourteen years old that spring and entered the last year of junior high school. Jonathon was now ten years old and looking more like his father every day. He had Charlie's clear green eyes, and even at this age, he was almost as tall as Heather.

Grandpa and Grandma Burbank came to spend the Christmas holidays with them. Anita watched Heather closely out of the corner of her eye and never missed an opportunity to hug her and tell her how much she loved her. It appeared to Heather that Grandpa Burbank's hair had gotten snowy white since the last time she had seen him, and was a tender, warm holiday; but Charlie's absence was very noticeable, and everybody was a little sad. Sometimes the memory of Charlie was so strong and clear that they all had to stop talking and be quiet for a little whilehe seemed to move a little slower.

One cold, crisp day, Stanford took Jonathon skiing while Anita, Heather, and Sara went shopping at the mall. They shopped and laughed and talked and giggled and had a great day! Grandma Anita bought Sara a pair of brown leather clogs and a soft sable-colored suede jacket to match. Heather was thrilled and felt very grown up.

Before she left for Connecticut, Anita took Heather to lunch one day. "So, Heather," she asked, "have you talked to the Lord about what kind of plans he has for your life?"

Heather just looked at her grandmother as if she had two heads. "Honestly, Grandma, sometimes the questions that you ask just don't seem to make any sense to me. How can I ask God questions if I am not even sure that I believe in him?"

Anita just looked right into Heather's eyes and replied, "But you won't always feel that way, Heather, and then all my questions will make sense. Remember the angels, sweetheart, they are always with you." Just then, the food arrived, and the subject was dropped, but of course not forgotten.

CHAPTER TWENTY-TWO

Growing Up

HEATHER WAS FIFTEEN YEARS OLD when she entered high school. This was a whole new world for her and her friends, Julie and Rebecca. Much of their time was spent studying, but in between, they did manage to talk about boys, fashion, and music. One night a week, they took turns studying at each others houses. Each had varied and distinguishing talents and likes and dislikes. Heather played the piano and Julie the flute. Rebecca was taking violin lessons but hadn't quite decided if she wanted to continue. Heather's favorite subjects were math and science, and Julie loved English and writing. Rebecca, on the other hand, was interested in history and the social sciences. They gleaned knowledge from each other and competed with each other for grades. However, they were always willing to help one another if one of them was having difficulty with a certain subject.

CHAPTER TWENTY-THREE

Surprises!

ONE COOL, FALL EVENING WHEN Heather arrived home from school, she noticed a brown Volvo in the driveway. She tried very hard to remember if she knew anyone with a car like that. The only person that came to her mind was Mr. Whitman, the math teacher at the junior high school, but even then, she wasn't sure.

Cautiously, she opened the front door and entered the hallway. Muffled voices and laughter were coming from the kitchen. She listened attentively. It really was the sound of her mother's laughter. Heather was a little surprised because she had not heard her mother laugh like that in a long time. Slowly and quietly, she tiptoed into the kitchen and peeked in.

Her mother and Paul Whitman were sitting at the kitchen table, drinking coffee and talking. All of a sudden, Heather felt as if someone had knocked the breath out of her.

She said quietly, "Hello, Mr. Whitman." And then she gave her mother a quizzical look, turned, left the kitchen, and walked upstairs to her room.

All through dinner, Heather refused to look at her mother. She helped her clear the table and put everything away, but she would not meet her mother's eyes. Mary Catharine came over about six thirty to take Jonathon to soccer practice. He and Julie's little sister, Lucy, were on the same team at the middle school; and Sara and Mary Catharine would take turns bringing them to the field.

Heather went upstairs to her room to do homework but noticed that Sara and Mary Catherine went into the kitchen for a while and talked in low tones. Later on that same night, when everyone was getting ready for bed, Sara quietly knocked on her daughter's door. She entered the room and sat down on the bed, where Heather was reading.

Thoughtfully and with great love and understanding, she looked deep into Heather's eyes. Heather could not turn away from her mother's face.

"Heather," Sara said, "you know that I love you and your brother very much, and that I have tried with all my heart and soul to give you both a normal life. We all had to endure a great loss, and I am so very proud of you and your brother, because it has taken great courage and perseverance to start new lives in the absence of your father.

Now I want to talk to you about Paul Whitman." When she said this, Heather lowered her head and refused to look at her mother. Sara sighed and took a deep breath, but was determined to continue. "We have known Paul Whitman for several years now. He is not a stranger to us. His parents live right next door, and when you were little, they used to help us out by taking care of you when your dad and I went out in the evening. Three years have now passed since your father's death, and sometimes, Heather, I must admit that I get a little lonely."

Finally, Heather looked up and said, "But you're not alone, Mother. You have us."

"Oh, Heather," Sara answered, "you are such a sweet and caring young girl. Please try to understand that a part of me will always grieve for your father, and no one can, and will, ever replace him. I loved him with all my being, and I will always love him, but I know that Charlie would not have wanted me to grieve forever. I know that he would have wanted me to have a friend, a companion."

Heather was aghast, and she blurted out, "Mom, you mean that you would actually go out on a date with Mr. Whitman, or have you already been dating him and keeping it a secret?" Heather could hear her voice breaking and could feel the hot, salty tears on her cheeks.

Sara replied, "No, Heather, I have not gone out on a date with anyone, but when the time comes, I want you to understand." Heather looked at her with tears streaming down her face. They looked at each other for a long moment. The air seemed pregnant with emotion. Then Sara gave Heather a quick hug and left the room.

Heather could not fall asleep that night. Her mind was filled with thoughts of her father. How could her mother do this? she thought. She felt betrayed and started to cry again. She muffled her sobs with her pillow and soon fell into a deep troubled sleep.

"Heather," a voice called to her. She sat up in bed and looked around the room. There was no one there. She lay back down and fell back to sleep.

"Heather," the voice called to her again. "Heather," the voice said again, "remember the angels." This time, she sat straight up in bed and turned on the light. There was no one in the room. She got out of bed and walked down the hallway to her mother's room. She opened the door and peeked in. Sara was sleeping peacefully with the moonlight shining on her face. Next, Heather walked to Jonathon's room and peeked in. Jonathon was fast asleep with all his covers on the floor. Heather walked in and gently covered him with the blankets. He stirred but didn't wake. Heather left his room and walked back to her own bedroom. She climbed into bed and turned off the light. As she was just beginning to fall asleep again, she felt a very warm and comforting presence envelope her. It was almost as if she was being held in someone's arms. Somehow it reminded her of her father.

CHAPTER TWENTY-FOUR

Paul

PAUL WHITMAN WAS NOT A tall man, perhaps only about five feet seven inches, with a rather stocky build. He worked out regularly at the local gym and rode his bike around the countryside on the weekends if he had time. He had deep blue eyes and straight sandy-colored hair, which he wore short, because when it grew too long, a lock of it always fell over his eyes and became bothersome. Whenever Paul moved, it was not quick or jerky. On the contrary, all his movements were slow and well calculated. He also planned his words carefully whenever he spoke, and if asked a difficult question, he thought for a long time before answering. He was a patient man and a good listener. But there was also something else about him that people noticed. He was an extremely gentle person and had almost an aura of kindness that followed him wherever he went. For this reason, adults as well as children, were attracted to him.

Paul, like Sara, had attended the University of Connecticut; but after graduation, he had decided to move to the South. Much to his parents' chagrin, in his senior year, he had become blindly enamored with a girl from Memphis, Tennessee. She had wanted to go back there after graduation, and so he followed.

The affair lasted about two years, and when it was over, Paul felt empty and bereft. However, he decided to stay in Memphis, where he was teaching at an inner city school. He found the work challenging and satisfying, and he was able to immerse himself in it and avoid thinking about his personal life.

He would visit his parents in Vermont twice a year, and sometimes they would also make the trek to the city of blues and music and enjoy all the sights and sounds. Paul was also a musician and moonlighted with a little band on the weekends. He met another girl, and it looked quite serious for a while. In fact, they almost became engaged; but somehow it didn't work out, and Paul remained single.

This went on for about eight years. Then one very humid Sunday morning, as he was walking to church, Paul decided that he missed New England very much. Why this happened after all this time, he would never know, but he began to dream about Vermont. He thought about the beautiful fall colors of the trees, the chilly prewinter nights when a fire crackled in the fireplace. He thought about the smells of cider and hot chocolate. He missed his parents. He missed the snow and the long afternoons spent on the slopes. He even missed the cold.

Wow, he thought to himself. *Maybe, I just need a good, long vacation.* He went on the Internet and tried to plan a vacation in the Caribbean, but he just couldn't bring himself to buy the ticket. *What is wrong with you, Paul?* he asked himself.

Finally, one Saturday morning, while he was drinking his coffee, he made a call to his parents. "Say, Mom and Dad," he said, "what would you think if I told you that I was thinking about moving back to New England?"

Well, his parents, Joyce and Michael, almost dropped the phone. Of course, they were overjoyed! The Whitmans were originally from Old Lyme, Connecticut, where Michael had worked as an insurance salesman for many years. Joyce had helped with the bookkeeping and also did bookkeeping for several other small businesses in the area. They had raised two children, Paul and Jocelyn. Jocelyn had gone to school in New York and was working for an investment broker. She, like Paul, had never married and seemed very content living in Manhattan and enjoying all the wonders of the big city. However, recently, she had mentioned to her parents that she was seeing someone special, and Joyce and Michael kept hoping that it would become serious. They perhaps felt that although Jocelyn always seemed to be cheerful and happy, they worried that maybe deep down inside, she was just a little bit lonely.

"It just so happens," Michael said to his son, "that I golf with a member of the school board on Wednesday mornings, and he recently confided in me that there are several openings for school teachers. Actually, one of them is a seventh-grade math position, which would be right down your alley."

Paul had to laugh at his parents' enthusiasm, but he was also pleased. He thought to himself that he was very lucky to have such loving, supportive parents. They had never stopped him from pursuing his own dreams, but they had always been there when he needed them. He knew that they had been very hurt when he left for Memphis, but had still continued to love him and had tried to respect his decisions. He knew that his parents were enjoying their retirement in Vermont. His father, he knew, had invested well; and although Joyce and Michael's life was not extravagant, he knew they needed very little.

"Well," he said to his dad, "do you think that you could get me an application? The school term ends in about a month, and I sure would like to have a job lined up before I make any big moves."

His father said that he would take care of it right away, and when he hung up the phone and turned to look at Joyce, he saw that she was smiling with tears in her eyes.

Paul applied for the teaching position, was interviewed on the telephone, and was hired for the seventh-grade math position. It all happened so fast that Paul wondered somehow if perhaps God had all this arranged before Paul even knew about it!

Paul moved in with his parents, who just happened to live next door to the Burbank family, and so he was very aware of all the happenings of that little family. His mother, Joyce, had on occasion helped with the care of the Burbank children. He had watched

Heather grow up and knew all about Jonathon's love for soccer from the stories his mother told him. He stayed with his parents for about eight months and then was able to purchase a little farm with about five acres of land on the outskirts of town. He thoroughly enjoyed working on his land. He refurbished the barn and bought two cows, some chickens, and ducks. He walked about the land and was followed around by a beautiful golden retriever named Molly and a stately German shepherd, who answered to the name of Henry. Paul felt good about his new life. The classes at the middle school were much smaller than the ones in Memphis, although the kids were every bit as challenging. Paul enjoyed reading and painting, but he did long for some female companionship at times, especially on those long, cold Vermont winter nights.

When he was living with his parents, Paul had seen Charlie and Sara playing games outside in the yard with their children, and he had commented to himself that they certainly were a very loving and wonderful family. He had also noticed what a beautiful woman Sara was. He thought that she looked great in a pair of jeans, and once in a while, he would catch a glimpse of Sara's wistful smile and thought to himself that Charlie was a very lucky man.

When Charlie began to get sick, Paul was already living on his little farm, and so he didn't get to see them very often. He knew, as everybody in the town did, that Charlie had become very ill; and he wondered how Sara was bearing up under all this. On several occasions, his mother shared her thoughts with him and she could only comment that Sara was a very brave woman and seemed to be holding up well.

When Charlie died, he and his parents attended the funeral together. Joyce was crying so much that she couldn't even say very much to Sara. He took it upon himself to walk up to Sara and offer his condolences. He looked into her eyes and saw a lot of pain, and all of a sudden, he just wanted to put his arms around her and to tell her that he was there for her; but he knew that this wouldn't be proper, so he just squeezed her hand and said a few words of sympathy and left.

CHAPTER TWENTY-FIVE

New Plans

ABOUT TWO YEARS HAD GONE by now, and he had only seen Sara in passing. Every once in a while, he would ask his mother about the Burbanks, and his mother would reply that Sara and the children seemed to keep themselves very busy. "Sara," she said, "is teaching at the grammar school, and Heather and Jonathon are very active in school activities. They have had to make a new life for themselves, and they seem to be succeeding, although sometimes when I look at Sara, I can tell that she misses Charlie very much. She is very resourceful and strong, but it's not easy to raise two children in this day and age!"

Paul commented that he thought he had seen Sara in the library when he went to the grammar school to get a particular math book that he had been looking for.

One snowy Friday evening, Paul stopped at the local market to pick up some provisions for the weekend. The weatherman on the radio was predicting snow for the weekend, and Paul chuckled to himself. *So what else is new?* he thought. He parked his car, entered the store, and grabbed a cart. As he was slowly walking down one of the isles, he looked up and noticed Sara. She was wearing a soft-looking pale blue sweater and jeans. Her blonde hair was shorter than he remembered it, but nevertheless, she looked lovely. She appeared to be having some difficulty with her grocery cart. The cart had a wobbly wheel and was making loud clumping noises when she pushed it. The wheels only turned slightly and then completely stopped. This was quite a predicament for her because the cart that she had was filled to the top with groceries. Swiftly, Paul left his cart and walked over to the front of the store and found an empty one for Sara. He walked up behind her with the cart, and she turned, startled. She was concentrating so hard on pushing the wagon that she did not notice him. Her expression at first registered surprise, then turned to a shy smile. She also noticed the empty cart that Paul had brought to her. "Why, Paul," she said, "how thoughtful of you." He had started to remove the groceries from her wagon and put them into the other when she protested. "Oh no, you don't have to do that, Paul. You were nice enough to bring me another wagon, but you don't have to help me move my groceries as well."

"But I want to," Paul replied as he continued to fill the cart. Sara then smiled and sighed and capitulated because she could see that he was quite determined. Together, they removed all her groceries from one cart to the other. A couple of times, when they were picking up cartons or food, their hands touched, and they laughed and kept on working. When the task was finished, Paul bowed and tipped his baseball cap and said, "It was a pleasure helping you, ma'am."

She looked at him and smiled, and then they both started laughing. Paul then turned, walked back to the end of the aisle where his cart was, and proceeded with his shopping. They saw each other at the checkout line, and he waited for her to be rung up. He then followed her to her car and helped her put the groceries in the back of the wagon. Sara was a little amazed at his attention, but decided that he was just being polite. However, as he was putting the last bag into the car, Paul totally surprised himself and her by asking, "Sara, would you consider going out to dinner with me?" He swallowed hard and could not believe that he had said that.

Sara drew her head back a little in astonishment. After a few seconds, however, she seemed to regain her composure. She smiled wistfully and slowly answered, "Well, Paul, I'd have to think about it for a while. After all, it's been a long time since I have been out on a date."

Paul looked into her face and said, "Well." He drew out the word slowly, "let's not think of it as a date, but rather, as two old friends sharing a meal together. Does that sound better?"

"Yes, it does," replied Sara with a little laugh. "But I'll tell you what, why don't you come over one day next week after school and have coffee at my house, and then perhaps we can catch up on old times and get to know each other better."

"Sounds great to me," Paul said, and they made a date for next Wednesday at four thirty in the afternoon. That was the earliest that Paul could get away since he coached the soccer team, and there was a practice every Wednesday.

Sara put this conversation out of her mind afterward because the weekend was so busy. She had to take Jonathon shopping on Saturday for new winter boots. It seemed that he had grown out of all his ski gear from last year also. Sara was sure that he was going to be tall like his father.

She also had to plan her lessons for next week, and she had totally forgotten that she had promised to teach church school for Ms. Patterson, who was out of town this weekend. She also had laundry to do and meals to prepare. She hoped that Heather would be able to help her with some of these chores. However, she knew that Heather was also very busy with all her friends, studies, and school activities. At the last minute, she decided to give Mrs. McCarthy a call and ask her for help.

"Of course, I'll come for a few hours while you are shopping with Jonathon. Don't you worry about a thing, Sara. I'll do the laundry and vacuum. That should help you a teeny bit, lass."

Sara was so grateful to her. "Thank you, God," she whispered. Well, the weekend was a blur; but surprisingly enough, when Sara awoke on Monday morning, she found that she was just a little bit apprehensive about Paul's visit but, deep down inside, just a little bit excited. "Maybe I should call and cancel," she said to herself several times, but somehow she never got around to doing that.

She found herself thinking about Charlie a lot also. *God, how I miss you Charlie*, she would find herself whispering.

CHAPTER TWENTY-SIX

Friendship

THAT PARTICULAR WEDNESDAY, JONATHON WAS visiting a friend after school, and Heather always stayed late to work on the school newspaper.

Sara found herself alone and was just a little bit nervous. Just before Paul was due to arrive, Sara chided herself. *What are you doing?* she asked herself. *How could you possibly invite someone you hardly know over to this house for coffee, especially a single man? Well*, she thought, *it's too late now. Besides, it's just coffee, and really, I have known him for several years now, so it's not like he is a perfect stranger!*

Just then, the doorbell rang, and Sara jumped and almost dropped the blueberry buckle that she was taking out of the oven. She put the cake on the table, smoothed her blouse, and then slowly walked to the door. She almost felt as if she was watching herself from afar. Something like an out of-body experience.

Paul Whitman waited outside the door, also feeling a little apprehensive. He wondered if perhaps he was making a mistake, but when Sara opened the door and he looked into her warm gray eyes, he knew in his heart that this was going to be okay.

"Come in," Sara said with a funny little laugh. "Come in, Paul."

She took his coat and hat and led him into the big living room, where a warm fire was blazing. She brought coffee and cake, and they both seated themselves on the comfortable old leather sofa. Time just seemed to fly by.

They embarked on a wonderful session of getting to know each other. Since they were both teachers, they, of course, had a lot in common. They found that they agreed on several methods of teaching, and they shared stories about their pupils and experiences. Paul fascinated Sara with tales of his teaching adventures in the South and the Southern culture.

Later, Paul helped her take the cups and dishes into the kitchen, where they both decided to sit at the table and continue talking. It was a warm and wonderful time of discovery for both of them, and they were both startled and a little embarrassed when Heather walked into the house.

LATER IN THE evening, when Paul was sitting on his front porch enjoying a glass of wine, he tried to put things into perspective. *What has caused this chain of events to happen?* he thought to himself. He was definitely attracted to Sara, that was a given, but he also had some reservations, because he had known, liked, and respected Charlie.

Should I pursue this relationship? he asked himself. *Or should I just leave things alone?*

Of course, in his heart, he knew the answer. He was going to pursue this relationship because he could not help himself. He was drawn to Sara and her family. *But,* he decided, *I will only pursue this on a friendship basis.*

CHAPTER TWENTY-SEVEN

Decisions

AND SO PAUL WHITMAN BECAME a good friend and helper to the Burbank family. He found himself especially drawn to Jonathon. Jonathon was a rugged, soft spoken young man with a head for math and soccer. Of course, these were subjects that Paul was very familiar with, and he found himself and Jonathon spending a lot of time together. At first, Sara was a little skeptical about the friendship; after all, she did not want her son to get hurt if Paul stopped coming around. She talked it over with Mary Catharine, who did not find anything unsettling about Paul. She encouraged Sara to just let things continue on their own, and so Sara did. After all, she knew that in her heart, she, like Jonathon, also enjoyed spendintime with Paul.

However, if Paul was making great headway with Jonathon, he definitely was not making any progress with Heather. It wasn't that Heather was rude to him or anything, it was just that she refused to acknowledge his growing presence in her family.

Sometimes, Paul would look up and find Heather just looking at him. It was a funny, quizzical look. It was as if she was trying to figure out what he could possibly mean to her mother and Jonathon.

She remained distant and aloof to him, and Paul realized that it was just going to take time.

Heather shared her resentment concerning Paul with her friends, but much to her chagrin, Julie and Rebecca did not agree with her.

"After all," Julie said one day, "your mom is a very attractive woman, Heather. Do you want her to remain a widow for the rest of her life?"

She also shared her feelings with Jamie, which was a big mistake because Jamie liked and admired Mr. Whitman very much. It became a sore point between them, and so Heather rarely brought the subject up.

CHAPTER TWENTY-EIGHT

Life Moves On

THANKSGIVING WAS JUST AROUND THE corner, and it brought a wonderful visit from Grandma Elizabeth and Uncle Aaron. One afternoon, Elizabeth and Heather went to Burlington to do a little shopping. They stopped at a little café for lunch, and Heather confided her feelings concerning Paul to her grandmother. She, of all people, would understand Heather's concern over the whole situation. She would certainly agree with Heather that perhaps her mother was surely having a nervous breakdown. Her grandmother listened intently as Heather poured out her frustrations. When Heather was finished, Elizabeth got up from her seat and came over to Heather, sat down beside her, and hugged her very hard. "Heather," she said, "do you think that Charlie—your wonderful, loving, giving father that we all loved so very much—would have wanted your mother to be alone for the rest of her life?"

"But she has Jonathon and me!" Heather protested. "Yes, yes," agreed Elizabeth, "but you and Jonathon are going to grow up one day and have lives of your own. After all, Heather, you will be going away to college in a couple of years, and Jonathon will someday also go away to school. You are a lovely and compassionate young woman, Heather, and we all are so very proud of you and love you very much. Why don't you try to show some of your love and understanding for your mother? Don't grow apart over this, Heather," her grandmother warned.

CHAPTER TWENTY-NINE

Confession

ONE SNOWY AFTERNOON IN EARLY December, Heather, Julie, and Rebecca had gathered at Rebecca's house to study for the midterms. It was grueling work because the girls were not easy on each other. Every question or math problem had to be investigated, dissected, and finally understood. Of course, it was great preparation for all of them, but also exhausting.

After partaking of cinnamon tea and delectable cookies that Rebecca's mom had baked, the girls decided to call it a day. Heather walked home with Julie; and just as she turned to leave, she saw Douglas, Julie's father, sweeping the freshly fallen snow from the front steps of the church. There was a meeting there tonight, and he was trying to keep the steps from getting too icy.

Douglas looked up and waved to Heather. "Hi, Heather," he called. "How's everything going? Julie tells me that you won an award for your science paper. Congratulations!"

"Thanks," she replied. "I really worked hard on that project, but I was very surprised when Mrs. Dwyer gave me that award."

"I just brewed a pot of tea, Heather. How about having a cup with me?" Heather hesitated a moment. Douglas coaxed, "It will warm you up for the walk home."

"Okay," Heather said as she followed him into his office. She put down her books and seated herself on the soft leather sofa in front of the little fireplace and inhaled the pungent smell of tea. Of course, this immediately reminded her of her father, and a sad look came over her face.

Douglas poured them each a cup of tea and seated himself comfortably in the large chair directly across from Heather.

"You've been awfully quiet lately, Heather, and you always look as if you've got a lot on your mind. Is there something that's troubling you? Would you like to talk about it? I know that I am the father of one of your best friends, but hopefully, I am also your friend and your priest."

Heather did not know or understand what happened to her at that particular moment. Maybe it was the smell of the tea or the concerned look in Douglas's eyes, or just the fact that she was tired of carrying all her unhappiness around. All of a sudden, she just started to talk, and she couldn't stop herself. She blurted out everything that she was feeling right then and there in that little office. She talked about her father's death and the strained relationship that she had with her mother at this time. She talked about Paul Whitman and the effect that he was having on her family and her disappointment with Jonathon because he was spending so much time with him. She told Douglas that she wanted everything back the way that it used to be. She wanted life to be like it was when her father was alive! She told him that she didn't believe in angels anymore. Then she started to cry. She cried and cried and cried until she felt that there were no more tears left in her. She felt embarrassed and silly, but she just couldn't help herself. It felt so good to just unload all this stuff!

Afterward, when she had finally stopped sniffling and was trying to gather her composure, Douglas got up from his chair and came over and gave her a hug. "Don't worry, Heather," he said, "I'll never breathe a word of this to anyone, not even Julie. But, Heather," he said, "I have a feeling that everything is going to turn out all right.

Just give this some time. Some times these situations work out just fine with some prayer and cooperation. Think about how your Dad would advise you. I know that you have doubts about God and the angels but don't give up on them completely, Next time you are feeling really down, try imagining that your Dad is sitting next to you on your bed or that old rocking chair of his in front of the fireplace. Tell him your troubles and then be still and listen. And Heather if you ever need to to talk with me again just come on over."

THAT NIGHT, WHEN Heather was huddled in her bed, just about to fall asleep, she thought that she heard someone say, "Remember the angels, Heather," but she was too exhausted to lift her head from the pillow; and besides, she didn't believe in angels anymore.

CHAPTER THIRTY

Present

"HEATHER," HER MOTHER CALLED, BRINGING the young girl out of her reverie, "Paul is here now. Come downstairs so that we can take some pictures."

Somewhat confused, Heather turned and glanced at her reflection in the mirror. She tried to clear her thoughts and bring herself back to the present time. Again, she heard her mother call. She walked from the room and closed the door behind her. As she walked slowly down the stairs, she saw her mother standing at the foot of them with a camera in her hand.

"Smile," Sara said as she snapped a picture. "Oh, Heather," Sara exclaimed, "you look so grown up. Your dad would be so proud of you. Sara's eyes began to glisten with tears as she quickly snapped another picture. Paul smiled and looked up at Heather and told her that she was going to be the belle of the ball. Her brother, Jonathon, had this strange look on his face and just kept staring at her as if he couldn't believe that this was really his sister.

The snow was falling harder now, and so Paul went outside to clean the windshield. Heather wrapped herself in the velvety red cape that her Grandmother Burbank had made her and followed her mother and her brother out the door. The snow was really falling heavily now and the truck skidded a little, before the tires grabbed the road, and they were off.

Everyone in the car was just a little excited and they all began talking at once. In all the excitement, they did not see the large semi truck that was barreling down the main street of the little town. All of a sudden bright lights shone into the car and blinded their eyes. The truck driver could not stop. The truck was skidding all over the road and appeared to be on target towards Paul's car.

Sara screamed as Paul desperately tried to stop the car by slowing down and stepping gently on the brakes. The truck was inches away from them when suddenly they were on the side of the road and the car was still. The big semi truck drove right past them. They couldn't understand what happened. They were all in shock and confusion. "What happened, they asked each other, over and over?" Everyone took a few minutes to make sure they were all alright. They were all relieved that they were all safe and sound. No one could understand what happened!!! After they all settled down, Heather said "It was just as if someone picked the car up and put it on the side of the road!" Then everyone began talking all at once coming up with all kinds of theories for this miracle and truly it was a miracle.

Paul was able to start the car and turn the heat back on. He drove off the side of the road onto the main road. It seemed that aside from everyone being a little shook up, all was back to normal, including the car. Paul, Sara, Heather and Jonathon were in total disbelief.

THEY DECIDED TO make a quick stop at Holloway's just to get themselves together and calm down a little bit.

The car drove without any problems to the little general store, where one could buy anything from a bottle of soda to a bicycle tire, and they all climbed out.

The bell above the door rang as they entered. The store was snug and warm and was to many people a place to congregate and discuss all sorts of things, and to others, it was a shelter in the storm. Mrs.

Holloway had the little pot bellied stove going, and when they shook their clothes to get rid of the snow, the droplets landed on the stove and made a hissing sound. Luckily, Sam Darwin, the Police Chief was also there, so Paul was able explain to him what happened. Sam was very surprised and almost speechless but he said that he was glad that no one was hurt and that he would look into it. He also added "When the snow stops falling, I will check out the area. However it would be rather hard to find the truck since no one was able to get a license plate number."

After that, everyone picked out the items that they wanted and leaned against the counter to be checked out. Mrs. Holloway had just baked some apple pies, and the aroma of apples and cinnamon filled the air. It reminded Heather of a Thanksgiving Day a long time ago.

Suddenly, the bell over the door rang again, and a man walked in. He had on a blue wool cap and a red-checked wool coat. His eyes were very green, with crinkly laugh lines around the edges. His red beard came just below his chin. He smiled and nodded hello to everyone. Heather was immediately filled with a strange sensation. There was something so very familiar about this man. It almost hurt to look at him. Her heart began to pound in her chest, and she had this overwhelming desire to rush over to the stranger and hug him. All of a sudden everything began to move in slow motion for Heather.

The stranger thoughtfully selected his articles and then took them to the counter. Mr. Holloway rang him up right away and put everything in a bag. Then the stranger did something very unusual. He turned to Sara, who had been watching him, and looked directly into her eyes for a long moment. Time seemed to stand still. Sara's gray eyes were held by the stranger's green eyes. Then the stranger turned very slowly toward Paul and smiled. He then walked over to Jonathon and gently placed a hand on his shoulder. "My, you've grown into a fine young man," he said. Then he stranger turned to look at Heather. Heather felt as if her heart and soul were going to burst from love and longing, and something else that was awesome and almost holy seemed to take place! What is happening? she asked herself. The hard rock of bitterness, anger, and hostility melted in

Heather; and suddenly, in her heart, she knew who the stranger was. His understanding, gentle green eyes met the intense, surprised look on her face. He smiled at her and exclaimed softly, "My goodness, young lady, don't you look like an enchanting angel tonight."

The stranger slowly turned back to the counter, picked up his bag, and walked toward the door. He turned once and looked at all of them and whispered, "Remember the angels." The little bell tinkled as the door closed.

HEATHER DID NOT really understand what happened that night, but it seemed as if when the stranger left, he took a part of her with him. Somehow her life was transformed that very night. Her thought processes became clearer, and she reached a new level of understanding. Her heart was no longer heavy. She felt lighter, happier, and even joyful. She wanted to laugh and jump up and down and turn cartwheels. She wanted to shout and tell everyone that she was okay, and that she believed in angels again. She went to the dance and, of course, had a lovely and magical time. Jamie kept asking her if she was all right because every now and then, she would start to giggle, and her eyes would dance with merriment. Heather would just smile and look at him. She wanted to savor this feeling within herself for as long as possible. Perhaps later on in their relationship, she would feel free to share her experience with Jamie, but not now.

In the days that followed, Heather's entire demeanor began to change. It was as if she had a sense of peace and harmony within herself. She knew beyond a doubt that yes, there were angels, and that one had visited them right here in Westford. She knew that her father was alive and well in a place that God had prepared for him. Most especially, she knew that she would never be alone because the angels would always be watching over her.

CHAPTER THIRTY-ONE

New Relationships

AS TIME PASSED, HEATHER AND Sara became friends again; and it was a deeper, kinder, more respectful relationship than it had ever been. Heather came to admire and understand her mother on a different level.

Heather also came to know and admire Paul Whitman. She, Sara, Jonathon, and Paul spent more time together, and the tension was gone. Dinners at home were fun again, and laughter and warmth returned to the house. They were becoming a family. Once in a while Joshua and Paige would also stop over and have dinner with them.

When Paul and Sara were married a year later, Heather and Jonathon were very happy and overjoyed to welcome Paul as part of their family. It was a lovely wedding at St. Lukes with Douglas officiating. The church was full of friends and three sets of grandparents all in attendance, especially the Whitmans who welcomed Heather and Jonathon as their own.

⊱✦⊰

AFTER MUCH DISCUSSION, Sara and Paul decided to continue to live at the house on Bridge Street. They would continue to do so until Jonathon left home for school, where ever that should turn out to be.

However, they spent many weekends and special holidays at the farm. On several occasions. Heather would invite Rebecca and Julie and all the girls would have great fun riding the horse and snuggling in front of the roaring fireplace in the "Keeping" room. Sometimes in the early morning, Heather would feel a wonderful and Holy presence in the room with her and she knew it was a very special angel. She kept this to herself for many years. Actually Heather had many experiences like this in the coming years.

CHAPTER THIRTY-TWO

The Future

EATHER'S HIGH SCHOOL YEARS CAME to an end and she went off to school in Boston, Massachusetts. Jonathon was looking at a college in Connecticut, maybe his father's alma mater.

The relationship between Heather and Jamie remained steadfast and true, although at times, they dated other people and they went through many trials and adventures together.

Many years later, however, they were to seal that bond with marriage. They were blessed with three children named Emily, Kate, and, of course, Charlie. Jamie's job took them traveling all over the country, even overseas, but no matter where they were, Heather always felt as if they were protected by an unseen circle of angels.

Sometimes, when it was still and quiet in the house and they were all sharing their special thoughts, Heather would always talk to her children about the angels, especially a green-eyed angel with a red beard. She would whisper to them, "Remember the angels, because they are always watching over you and protecting you. Sometimes they may even communicate with you in a very special way, but you must be open to them and trust and listen. When you go through those difficult and sad times in your life, as we all do, pray and ask God and his angels to help you. Even when you make mistakes and end up in a challenging situation. Never give up. You will be guided and directed, and the angels will show you the way. Keep an open mind.

Heather had many experiences with angels in her lifetime, and there are many stories that can be told about those experiences. However, this story is just the beginning.

THE END

www.ingramcontent.com/pod-product-compliance
Lightning Source LLC
Chambersburg PA
CBHW020330130626
46549CB00003B/1106